I0698007

The 100 miles that matters alot for diabetes cookbook

The significance of a specific distance in terms of physical activity and lifestyle for managing diabetes

By

Janet Ryles

Copyright © Katherine Martin 2023

All Rights Reserved

Table of contents

- Culinary Reflections: Making Every Meal Count
- Continuing the Journey Beyond "The 100 Miles"

Each chapter in "The 100 Miles That Matters Lot for Diabetes Cookbook" is designed to guide you through a culinary exploration that aligns with the principles of diabetes care and wellness.

Introduction

Welcome to "The 100 Miles That Matters Alot for Diabetes Cookbook," a culinary companion meticulously crafted for those navigating the intricate landscape of diabetes management. In these pages, we embark on a flavorful journey, transcending the ordinary to discover the extraordinary impact of nutrition on your well-being. Beyond the symbolic significance of a hundred miles, we delve into a world where every ingredient, every recipe, is a conscious step toward balance and vitality.

This cookbook isn't just about meals; it's a roadmap to making dietary choices that resonate with the principles of diabetes care. With a fusion of delectable recipes and evidence-based nutritional guidance, we invite you to explore a palate of possibilities that harmonize taste and health. Each dish is a celebration, a testament to the idea that the journey to wellness is as delicious as it is significant.

Whether you're a seasoned chef or a novice in the kitchen, "The 100 Miles That Matters Alot for Diabetes Cookbook" is your compass for creating meals that align with your health goals. Embrace the art of mindful eating, savor the flavors of well-being, and let this cookbook be your trusted companion on the path to a healthier, more vibrant life. Get ready to redefine your relationship with food and make every culinary endeavor a stride toward diabetes wellness.

In the pursuit of optimal diabetes management, embark on a transformative journey with "The 100 Miles That Matters Alot for Diabetes." This compelling guide unveils the power of a hundred miles—a symbolic threshold where lifestyle choices intersect with well-being. Dive into a narrative that transcends mere distance, exploring the pivotal role of physical activity in diabetes care. Discover actionable insights, expert advice, and inspirational stories that illuminate the path to health, one step at a time. Join us on a quest where each mile isn't just a number but a meaningful stride towards a brighter, healthier future. Are you ready to redefine the way you approach diabetes and make every mile count.

Chapter One

Nourishing Foundations Building a Diabetes-Friendly Pantry:

In this foundational chapter, we lay the groundwork for your journey toward healthier eating habits. We delve into the essential elements of a diabetes-friendly pantry, guiding you in selecting ingredients that align with optimal blood sugar control. From whole grains to lean proteins and heart-healthy fats, we explore the building blocks that form the basis of nutritious and delicious meals.

Key Topics:

1. Understanding Glycemic Index (GI): Unravel the concept of GI and its impact on blood sugar levels. Learn how to make informed choices when selecting carbohydrates to maintain stable glucose levels.

2. Fiber-Rich Essentials: Explore the world of fiber and its role in promoting digestive health and regulating blood sugar. Discover pantry staples that are rich in soluble and insoluble fiber.

3. Smart Sugar Substitutes: Delve into alternative sweeteners that add sweetness without the glycemic spike. Understand how to incorporate them

into recipes while maintaining flavor balance.

4. Heart-Healthy Fats: Learn about the importance of incorporating healthy fats into your diet for overall well-being. Discover sources of omega-3 fatty acids and monounsaturated fats that support cardiovascular health.

Practical Tips:

- *Label Reading:* Equip yourself with the skills to decipher nutrition labels. Identify hidden sugars and make informed choices while grocery shopping.

- *Meal Planning:* Embrace the art of meal preparation by stocking your pantry with versatile and wholesome ingredients. We provide practical tips for efficient meal planning, making it easier to maintain a diabetes-conscious diet.

Recipes:

Experience the application of pantry essentials with a selection of beginner-friendly recipes. From a fiber-rich quinoa salad to a hearty lentil soup, these recipes showcase the diversity and deliciousness of diabetes-friendly ingredients.

By the end of Chapter 1, you'll have the knowledge and tools to transform your pantry into a diabetes-conscious culinary haven, setting the stage for a journey filled with nourishing and flavorful meals.

Chapter Two

Breakfasts That Energize Balanced Morning Starters within the "100 Miles" Framework:

Welcome to the heart of your day – breakfast. In this chapter, we explore the critical role of a well-balanced morning meal in kickstarting your day while aligning with the principles of "The 100 Miles." We delve into the synergy between wholesome ingredients and energy-boosting breakfast options that contribute to stable blood sugar levels.

Key Topics:

1. Protein-Packed Breakfasts:
   Understand the significance of
   incorporating protein into your
   morning routine. Explore diverse
   protein sources, including eggs, Greek
   yogurt, and plant-based alternatives, to
   fuel your day effectively.

2. Whole Grains for Sustained Energy:
   Discover the power of whole grains in
   providing long-lasting energy and
   stabilizing blood sugar. From oats to
   quinoa, we guide you in incorporating
   these grains into delicious breakfast
   creations.

3. Balancing Carbohydrates: Learn how
   to strike a balance with carbohydrates,
   choosing complex carbs that release

energy gradually, preventing spikes in blood sugar levels. Explore creative ways to enjoy carbs without compromising nutritional value.

4. Mindful Breakfast Choices: Embrace mindfulness in your morning routine. We discuss the importance of being present during meals and savoring each bite, fostering a positive relationship with food.

Practical Tips:

- *Preparation Techniques:* Gain insights into efficient breakfast preparation techniques for busy mornings. Discover make-ahead options and quick recipes that fit seamlessly into your daily routine.

- *Customization for Dietary Preferences:* Whether you follow a vegetarian, vegan, or omnivorous diet, we provide tips on customizing breakfast options to suit various dietary preferences while still meeting diabetes-conscious criteria.

Recipes:

Explore a collection of enticing breakfast recipes tailored to meet the needs of those managing diabetes. From a protein-packed breakfast bowl to a fiber-rich smoothie, each recipe is crafted to invigorate your morning while supporting your health goals.

By the end of Chapter 2, you'll have a repertoire of nutritious and delicious breakfast ideas, setting a positive tone for

your day and embracing the principles of
"The 100 Miles That Matters Alot for
Diabetes Cookbook."

Chapter Three

Satisfying Snacks for the Journey Mindful Munching: Snacks That Support Diabetes Wellness:

In this chapter, we explore the world of snacks, navigating the balance between satisfying cravings and maintaining blood sugar stability. From quick bites to portable options, discover a plethora of snack ideas designed to align with the principles of "The 100 Miles."

Key Topics:

1. Balancing Macronutrients in Snacks: Understand the importance of

incorporating a balance of carbohydrates, proteins, and fats into your snacks. Learn how this combination can provide sustained energy and prevent rapid blood sugar fluctuations.

2. Portion Control and Smart Snacking: Delve into the concept of mindful eating and portion control. Discover strategies to enjoy snacks in moderation while avoiding overconsumption, a crucial aspect of diabetes management.

3. Snacking on Whole Foods: Embrace the idea of snacking on whole, minimally processed foods. Explore

nutrient-dense options that contribute to overall health and well-being.

4. Portable Snacks for On-the-Go: Whether you're at work, traveling, or simply on the move, we provide a variety of snack ideas that are convenient, portable, and conducive to a busy lifestyle.

Practical Tips:

- *Snack Planning for Stability:* Develop a personalized snack plan to maintain blood sugar stability throughout the day. We offer practical tips on prepping snacks in advance and keeping healthy options readily available.

- *Smart Substitutions:* Explore ingredient substitutions and snack alternatives that cater to your taste preferences while adhering to diabetes-conscious choices.

Recipes:

Indulge in a selection of snack recipes crafted to satiate cravings without compromising on nutritional value. From crunchy roasted chickpeas to a refreshing Greek yogurt parfait, these recipes showcase the diversity and creativity of diabetes-friendly snacks.

By the end of Chapter 3, you'll have the tools to navigate snack choices with confidence, incorporating delicious options into your routine that align with the principles of "The 100 Miles That Matters Alot for Diabetes Cookbook."

Chapter Four

Wholesome Soups and Salads Soups Packed with Flavor and Nutrition:

In this chapter, we explore the world of wholesome soups and salads, showcasing the versatility and health benefits of incorporating nutrient-dense ingredients. From comforting soups to vibrant salads, discover culinary delights that align with the principles of "The 100 Miles."

Key Topics:

1. Balancing Flavors in Soups: Explore the art of crafting soups that are both delicious and diabetes-friendly. Learn

how to balance flavors while using ingredients that contribute to overall health.

2. The Power of Broths: Delve into the nutritional benefits of broths as a foundation for soups. From bone broth to vegetable broth, understand how these bases can enhance the nutrient content of your soups.

3. Incorporating Whole Grains and Legumes: Discover the heartiness of whole grains and legumes in soups, adding texture, fiber, and essential nutrients. From quinoa to lentils, explore a variety of options that contribute to a balanced diet.

4. Creative Salad Combinations: Elevate your salad game with creative combinations of fresh produce, lean proteins, and flavorful dressings. Learn how to make salads that are not only nutritious but also satisfying and enjoyable.

Practical Tips:

- *Batch Cooking for Convenience:* Embrace the convenience of batch-cooking soups and salads. Learn how to prepare larger quantities and store them for quick and easy meals throughout the week.

- *Balancing Ingredients for Nutrient Density:* Gain insights into balancing ingredients to maximize the nutritional density of your soups and salads. Discover the synergy between various components to create wholesome and satisfying meals.

Recipes:

Immerse yourself in a collection of soup and salad recipes that showcase the diverse flavors and textures of these dishes. From a hearty minestrone to a refreshing avocado and quinoa salad, each recipe is crafted to delight your taste buds while supporting your health goals.

By the end of Chapter 4, you'll have the inspiration and knowledge to create nourishing soups and salads that align with the principles of "The 100 Miles That

Matters Alot for Diabetes Cookbook,"
enhancing your table's taste and wellness.

Chapter Five

Main Courses That Matter Exploring Diabetes-Friendly Proteins and Plant-Based Options:

In this pivotal chapter, we dive into the heart of your meals – the main courses. Discover a variety of plant-based and diabetes-friendly proteins that can satisfy your hunger and help you maintain stable blood sugar levels by the guidelines of "The 100 Miles."

Key Topics:

1. Lean Proteins for Diabetes Care: Understand the role of lean proteins in maintaining energy levels and

supporting muscle health. From poultry to fish and plant-based protein sources, explore diverse options suitable for diabetes management.

2. Plant-Powered Main Courses: Delve into the world of plant-based main courses that celebrate the richness of vegetables, legumes, and grains. Learn how to create satisfying plant-based meals that are both flavorful and nutritious.

3. Balancing Carbohydrates in Main Courses: Explore strategies for balancing carbohydrates in your main courses to prevent rapid spikes in blood sugar. Discover how pairing

carbs with fiber-rich foods can contribute to better glycemic control.

4. Incorporating Whole Foods: Embrace the philosophy of using whole, minimally processed ingredients in your main courses. Learn how these choices contribute not only to diabetes wellness but also to overall health and vitality.

Practical Tips:

- *Meal Planning for Variety:* Gain insights into meal planning to ensure a diverse range of main courses throughout the week. Discover how variety can keep your meals interesting while providing a broad spectrum of nutrients.

- *Cooking Techniques for Retaining Nutrients:* Explore cooking techniques that preserve the nutritional value of ingredients. From steaming to roasting, understand how different methods can enhance the flavors and health benefits of your main courses.

Recipes:

Immerse yourself in a collection of main course recipes that showcase the delicious possibilities within the realm of diabetes-conscious eating. From a grilled lemon herb chicken to a hearty lentil and vegetable stew, each recipe is crafted to bring both satisfaction and nutrition to your table.

By the end of Chapter 5, you'll have the knowledge and inspiration to create main courses that not only matter to your taste buds but also contribute significantly to your diabetes wellness journey.

Chapter Six

Smart Sides and Accompaniments Balanced Side Dishes to Complement Your Meals:

In this chapter, we explore the art of creating smart side dishes and accompaniments that harmonize with your main courses, contributing to a well-rounded and diabetes-conscious culinary experience within the framework of "The 100 Miles."

Key Topics:

1. Vegetable-Centric Sides: Dive into the world of vibrant, nutrient-packed vegetables that form the foundation of

smart side dishes. Discover creative cooking techniques and flavor combinations to elevate the appeal of vegetables on your plate.

2. Whole Grains as Accompaniments: Explore the diversity of whole grains as accompaniments to your meals. From quinoa to farro, understand how these grains not only add texture and flavor but also contribute essential nutrients and fiber.

3. Healthy Fats in Side Dishes: Embrace the role of healthy fats in enhancing the taste and nutritional value of your sides. Learn about sources of monounsaturated fats and omega-3 fatty acids that can be incorporated

into side dishes to support overall
health.

4. Balancing Flavors and Textures:
   Understand the importance of
   balancing flavors and textures in side
   dishes to create a satisfying dining
   experience. Explore the interplay
   between savory, sweet, and umami
   elements to enhance your meals.

Practical Tips:

- *Pairing Strategies:* Gain insights into
  pairing side dishes with main courses
  to create complementary and balanced
  meals. Discover strategies for
  achieving harmony in flavors and
  nutritional content.

- *Efficient Cooking for Busy Schedules:*
  Explore time-saving cooking
  techniques and recipes that allow you
  to prepare delicious and nutritious side
  dishes even on the busiest days.

Recipes:

Immerse yourself in a collection of side dish
recipes that showcase the versatility and
creativity of accompaniments within the
diabetes-conscious framework. From a
roasted vegetable medley to a quinoa and
black bean salad, each recipe is crafted to
elevate your meals with both taste and
nutritional value.

By the end of Chapter 6, you'll have the
tools to create side dishes that not only
complement your main courses but also

contribute significantly to the overall
balance and satisfaction of your
diabetes-conscious culinary journey.

Chapter Seven

Sweet Endings Desserts Redefined: Satisfying the Sweet Tooth Mindfully:

In this delightful chapter, we embark on a journey to redefine desserts within the framework of diabetes management. Explore the sweet side of a diabetes-conscious lifestyle, discovering ways to satisfy your cravings while maintaining optimal blood sugar levels.

Key Topics:

1. Mindful Sugar Substitutes: Delve into the world of sugar substitutes that cater to your sweet tooth without

causing spikes in blood sugar. Learn
about natural alternatives and how to
incorporate them into your favorite
dessert recipes.

2. Incorporating Fruits in Desserts:
Discover the natural sweetness of
fruits as a key component in
diabetes-friendly desserts. From
berries to citrus, explore a variety of
fruits that add flavor, color, and
nutritional value to your sweet
creations.

3. Balancing Carbohydrates: Understand
the importance of balancing
carbohydrates in desserts to prevent
rapid blood sugar fluctuations. Explore
ways to incorporate fiber-rich

ingredients that contribute to better glycemic control.

4. Portion Control and Indulgence: Learn the art of portion control and mindful indulgence. Discover strategies for enjoying desserts in moderation, making them a delightful part of your culinary experience without compromising your health goals.

Practical Tips:

- *Baking Techniques for Diabetes-Friendly Desserts:* Explore baking techniques and ingredient substitutions that allow you to create delicious desserts with a lower impact on blood sugar. Discover the

versatility of almond flour, coconut
flour, and other alternatives.

- *Creative Presentation:* Elevate the
presentation of your desserts for a
visually appealing experience. Learn
how to garnish and plate your sweet
creations to make them both enticing
and satisfying.

Recipes:

Immerse yourself in a collection of dessert
recipes designed to redefine the sweet
ending to your meals. From a berry and
almond crumble to a dark chocolate avocado
mousse, each recipe is crafted to bring joy to
your taste buds while aligning with the
principles of The Diabetes Cookbook: The
100 Miles That Matters a Lot."

By the end of Chapter 7, you'll have the knowledge and inspiration to enjoy sweet endings mindfully, making desserts a delightful and integral part of your diabetes-conscious culinary journey.

Chapter Eight

Beverages Beyond Borders Hydration and Flavor Infusions:

In this refreshing chapter, we explore the diverse world of beverages, emphasizing hydration and flavor without compromising diabetes-conscious choices. From infused waters to warm beverages, discover a spectrum of options that elevate your drink choices within the principles of "The 100 Miles."

Key Topics:

1. Importance of Hydration: Delve into the crucial role of hydration in

diabetes management. Understand the impact of adequate water intake on overall well-being and blood sugar regulation.

2. Diabetes-Friendly Drinks: Explore a variety of beverages that cater to different tastes while aligning with the principles of managing diabetes. From herbal teas to naturally flavored water, discover options that are both hydrating and enjoyable.

3. Balancing Sugars in Beverages: Learn how to make informed choices regarding sugary beverages, and understand the impact of different sweeteners on blood sugar levels. Discover alternatives and strategies for

creating refreshing drinks without excessive added sugars.

4. Nutrient-Packed Smoothies: Explore the world of nutrient-packed smoothies that combine flavors and health benefits. Learn how to create satisfying and diabetes-friendly blends that can serve as convenient meal replacements or snacks.

Practical Tips:

- *Infusions and Flavor Pairing:* Gain insights into flavor infusions and creative pairings that enhance the taste of your beverages naturally. From cucumber mint water to ginger lemon tea, discover combinations that are both delicious and health-conscious.

- *Portion Control for Caloric Beverages:* Understand the importance of portion control, especially when it comes to caloric beverages. Learn how to enjoy flavorful drinks in moderation while keeping an eye on overall calorie and sugar intake.

Recipes:

Immerse yourself in a collection of beverage recipes designed to quench your thirst while aligning with diabetes-conscious choices. From a refreshing green tea and berry infusion to a nutrient-packed green smoothie, each recipe is crafted to elevate your hydration experience.

By the end of Chapter 8, you'll have a repertoire of beverage choices that not only keep you hydrated but also contribute to the overall enjoyment of your meals within the concepts outlined in "The Diabetes Cookbook: The 100 Miles That Matters a Lot."

Chapter Nine

Celebrations and Gatherings Hosting Events with Diabetes-Considerate Menus:

In this festive chapter, we explore the art of hosting events and gatherings while keeping diabetes management at the forefront. Discover strategies for creating menus that celebrate special occasions without compromising health goals within the principles of "The 100 Miles."

Key Topics:

1. Planning Diabetes-Friendly Menus: Delve into the process of planning menus for celebrations and gatherings

that cater to diverse tastes while aligning with diabetes-conscious choices. Understand how to create a well-balanced spread that includes a variety of flavors and textures.

2. Interactive Cooking and Serving: Explore the concept of interactive cooking and serving, where guests can participate in creating their meals. Learn how this approach not only adds an element of fun to gatherings but also allows individuals to make choices that suit their dietary needs.

3. Special Occasion Treats: Discover ways to incorporate special occasion treats into your menus while maintaining a focus on diabetes

wellness. From desserts to festive beverages, explore creative and mindful choices that everyone can enjoy.

4. Navigating Social Dining: Understand how to navigate social dining situations, whether at home or in a restaurant setting. Learn communication strategies to ensure your dietary needs are met without making the event solely about diabetes.

Practical Tips:

- *Communication with Guests:* Gain insights into communicating with guests about dietary preferences and restrictions. Learn how to create an inclusive environment where everyone feels comfortable and accommodated.

- *Event Planning Timeline:* Explore a timeline for event planning that includes considerations for menu preparation, shopping, and cooking. Discover how a well-organized approach can reduce stress and enhance the overall experience.

Recipes:

Immerse yourself in a collection of recipes designed for celebrations and gatherings, ranging from appetizers to desserts. From a colorful vegetable platter with yogurt dip to a light and refreshing fruit sorbet, each recipe is crafted to bring joy to special occasions while respecting diabetes-conscious choices.

By the end of Chapter 9, you'll have the knowledge and tools to host events that are not only festive and enjoyable but also considerate of diabetes management, making every celebration a memorable and health-conscious experience.

Chapter Ten

Fitness Fuel Connecting Culinary Choices with Physical Activity:

In this dynamic chapter, we explore the intricate connection between culinary choices and physical activity, emphasizing the role of nutrition in supporting a healthy and active lifestyle within the principles of "The 100 Miles."

Key Topics:

1. Understanding Nutrient Timing: Delve into the concept of nutrient timing—aligning your meals with your physical activity. Explore how pre-and

post-workout nutrition can enhance performance, aid recovery, and support overall well-being.

2. Balancing Macronutrients for Energy: Explore the importance of balancing macronutrients—carbohydrates, proteins, and fats—to provide the energy needed for various types of physical activity. Learn how different activities may require adjustments in your dietary approach.

3. Hydration for Optimal Performance: Understand the critical role of hydration in physical activity. Explore the impact of water and electrolyte balance on performance and recovery,

and learn strategies for staying properly hydrated.

4. Nutrient-Dense Snacking for Active Lifestyles: Discover the art of nutrient-dense snacking for sustained energy during physical activities. Learn about portable snacks that can fuel your workouts and keep you energized throughout the day.

Practical Tips:

- *Meal Planning for Active Days:* Gain insights into meal planning strategies for days with increased physical activity. Understand how to tailor your meals to provide the necessary fuel for workouts and promote recovery.

- *Choosing Foods for Endurance vs. Strength Training:* Explore the different nutritional needs for endurance-based activities and strength training. Learn how to adjust your diet to meet the specific demands of your fitness routine.

Recipes:

Immerse yourself in a collection of recipes designed to fuel your active lifestyle. From pre-workout energy bites to post-workout recovery smoothies, each recipe is crafted to provide the nutrients your body needs for optimal performance and recovery.

By the end of Chapter 10, you'll have a comprehensive understanding of how culinary choices can support your physical activity, creating a synergy between your diet and fitness routine within the concepts outlined in "The Diabetes Cookbook: The 100 Miles That Matters a Lot."

Conclusion chapter

As we reach the culmination of "The 100 Miles That Matters Alot for Diabetes Cookbook," it's time to reflect on the journey we've embarked upon—a journey that goes beyond mere recipes and culinary techniques. This cookbook is not just about food; it's a testament to the profound connection between our choices and our well-being, especially when managing diabetes.

Key Reflections:

1. Empowerment through Knowledge: Throughout these pages, we've delved into the nuances of diabetes-conscious eating, exploring the significance of ingredients, portion control, and

mindful choices. Knowledge has been the cornerstone of empowerment, enabling you to make informed decisions that align with your health goals.

2. Culinary Creativity and Diversity: From breakfast to dessert, soups to snacks, each chapter has been a canvas for culinary creativity and diversity. The recipes showcased here celebrate the rich tapestry of flavors and textures within the boundaries of diabetes-conscious choices.

3. Balancing Act: "The 100 Miles" is not just a symbolic distance; it's a metaphor for balance. We've learned to balance macronutrients, flavors, and

culinary experiences, making every meal a mindful and balanced act that contributes to overall health.

Continuing the Journey:

As you close this cookbook, remember that your journey doesn't end here—it's an ongoing exploration of health and well-being. Use the knowledge gained within these pages as a foundation for continued growth and adaptation. Keep experimenting with new ingredients, trying out different recipes, and discovering the joy in crafting meals that matter.

Staying Connected:

Join our community of individuals committed to diabetes-conscious living. Share your experiences, ask questions, and inspire others on similar journeys. Whether through social media, online forums, or local support groups, staying connected fosters a sense of community and mutual support.

Gratitude:

A heartfelt thank you for choosing "The 100 Miles That Matters Lot for Diabetes Cookbook." It has been our pleasure to guide you on this culinary adventure. May your meals be not only delicious but also a source of vitality and wellness. Here's to a future filled with flavorful choices, mindful eating, and the continued pursuit of a healthier, happier you.

www.ingramcontent.com/pod-product-compliance
Lightning Source LLC
Chambersburg PA
CBHW060210260726

48658CB00005BA/1978